Speed Reading

How to Increase Reading Speed with
Speed Reading Techniques, Learn Faster
and be More Productive

Kevin Thomson

with express written consent from the Publisher. All additional right reserved.

The information in the following pages is broadly considered to be a truthful and accurate account of facts and as such any inattention, use or misuse of the information in question by the reader will render any resulting actions solely under their purview. There are no scenarios in which the publisher or the original author of this work can be in any fashion deemed liable for any hardship or damages that may befall them after undertaking information described herein.

Additionally, the information in the following pages is intended only for informational purposes and should thus be thought of as universal. As befitting its nature, it is presented without assurance regarding its prolonged validity or interim quality. Trademarks that are mentioned are done without written consent and can in no way be considered an endorsement from the trademark holder.

Table of Contents

Introduction

The following chapters will discuss several techniques and reasons for speed reading. Speed reading doesn't mean you skim through the text and not understand what you just read. Speed reading means you extract the most important information so that you comprehend what you are reading without taking as much time.

This book will take you through the history of speed reading so that you can understand that it's not some new fad to make life easier. You will also learn how speed reading can help you in many different aspects of your life. The average reader reads around 200 words per minute and they only comprehend about 60 percent of what they read. Top speed readers can average 1000 words per minute and they can comprehend about 85 percent of what they read.

It just goes to show you that speed reading will improve your comprehension and not take away from it.

After you have learned the importance of speed reading, we'll go into different ways to speed up your reading. There are lots of different ways to up your reading speed and to test your own reading speed.

This process can be extremely fun to do, especially if you like reading. And I'm guessing you probably do, otherwise, you wouldn't be here. The average person reads slower because they verbalize each word in their head. This means that you are reading at the same pace that you talk. Your brain is able to read faster than that if you would just let it.

Now, just because you are learning how to speed read doesn't mean you will have to all the time. There is a time and place for speed reading. If you are reading important legal documents, business reports, or the like, you probably don't want to speed read those. You can choose when and where to use your speed reading skills.

This is a helpful skill to have in your back pocket. Let's get started.

There are plenty of books on this subject on the market, thanks again for choosing this one! Every effort was made to ensure it is full of as much useful information as possible, please enjoy!

The History of Speed Reading

A natural trait of humans is that we all gather information. It only makes it natural that after we learn how to read, we want to do it faster so that we are able to absorb and gather more information.

The United States Air Force created one of the first insights into speed reading using the methodology that had been used for the tachistoscope. This was a device that was able to display an image for a certain length of time, and then it quickly takes it away. This device was being used as a training device for pilots so that they could quickly identify enemy planes while flying. With a bit of experimentation, they found that a reader could understand four words that were shown on the screen for 500th of a second.

They originally thought that people read by paying attention to each letter that was in a word in order so that they could understand the meaning. The experiments performed by the U.S. Air Force changes this idea of having to read each letter, and it was able to help create the understanding that humans can read more than a single word at a time.

Oddly enough, besides these studies performed by the US Air Force in 1925 at Syracuse University, there hasn't been very much support from governments or educational establishments. You would think that there would be academic plaudits or increased attainments to be gained by the first country or organization to start implementing a reading program that would take students further than the basics. All of the advances, though, seem to only have been made by individuals who were committed to reading faster and have remained outside formal education, and this is still true today.

One interviewer asked Bill Gates in an interview, "If you could have one superpower what would it be?" His answer was, "The ability to read super fast."

Most of these individual innovations have been accepted in the field, but even in this "field," most people are still unaware of the advances and work of others, so it is probable that there are "discoveries" that have been made by several people. Many of the techniques that people have come up with have remained unique to the creator, and there are some that could have flourished for a moment but have been lost. So this chapter is going to look at a partial, incomplete history of speed reading ideas.

Earliest References

In the third part of the 19th century, there were some early references to speed reading, albeit, speed reading wasn't the way it was described. Emil Javel, around 1878, was a French ophthalmologist who is best remembered for the work he did on correcting squints. He performed experiments into the way the eye worked when a person was reading. He was the one that stated that the eyes perform a series of jumps, known as saccades, along a line and will then pause to consume the information at different stops, known as fixation.

He also found that it was possible for a person to take in information from either side of the fixation. This means that people were able to understand chunks of text, instead of having to read each word. Around six years later, articles started showing up in journals about improved reading skills that people could gain from reading groups of words that weren't vocalized.

Then information about speed reading went quiet for a few decades until around 1921. This is when John Anthony O'Brien wrote his book called, *"Silent Reading: with special reference to methods for developing speed, a study in the psychology and pedagogy of reading."* This book reiterated the idea that it was possible for people to read groups of words without vocalizing them in their head.

Harvard University started performing experiments in the 1940s on rapid reading using a tachistoscope. They used this to encourage recognition speed. This meant that it could be used to help participants increase or test their speed of reading. It was also able to show items for such a short amount of time that a person couldn't consciously register them. This information would probably be useful for experiments on what is known as downloading, which is also called PhotoReading.

Mortimer Adler

It's important to know that in the book *How to Read a Book* was published in 1940 by an American professor, educator, and philosopher theorist, Dr. Mortimer J Adler. The original book had more to do about classifying books and how they need to be read in depth instead of reading them faster. However, in the 1966 revised edition, he talks about syntopical reading, which is the basis of comparative reading many books with a single purpose at a single time. He defines this as "reading in" the entire set of books instead of just "reading through" a single book.

Adler decided that the set of great books were those that he had extracted the ideas on what western civilization is based. These ideas were indexed and known as Syntopicon. He hoped that readers would use these to compare the thoughts of all the great thinkers from the past 3000 years in just moments. If you are interested in finding out what these were, a quick Google search will give everything you need to know.

You can find the 72 authors from which he formed his ideas in "Great Books of the Western World." Adler, for the majority of these authors, recommends more than a single book, and for many of them, which include Sophocles, Archimedes, Hippocrates, and Shakespeare, he suggests that you read their complete works.

These are all supplemented by an extra 153 listed under a heading "Gateway to the Great Books."

Adler also believed in holistic reading, or what was sometimes known as "global to detail" reading. He wrote, "To understand a book, you must approach it, first, as a whole, having a unity and a structure of part; and second, in terms of its elements, its units of language and thought." He also believed that you should keep an open mind: "Understanding an author must always precede criticizing or judging him."

Evelyn Wood

Evelyn Wood brought speed reading to the attention of the people in the US in the late 1950s. She was the one who coined the term "speed reading" before it became popular. Her book *Reading* Skills was published in 1959. She was originally a school teacher. During her time as a school teacher, she studied the habits of those who were naturally fast readers and then came up with a methodology that she taught in seminars through the country. Her studies looked at people who were able to read 1500 to 6000 words a minute. They often read down the page instead of side to side, which is known as super-reading. She also found that faster readers tended to be more effective and efficient. She even studied President John F. Kennedy. Colleges taught her method of speed until the late '90s throughout the US. She passed away at the age of 86 in 1995.

With help from her husband, she came up with a system that increased a person's reading speed, on average, by a factor of two to five times more, with an increase in retention. This was named the Evelyn Wood Speed Reading Dynamics. Members of the White House staff took her courses. She has been credited with introducing the pacer method.

Throughout the years, the techniques for speed reading have been refined, but the foundations are still the same. The basics of speed reading involve reading several words at once without internally vocalizing—known as subvocalizing—the words. Subvocalization is something that you won't be able to get rid of completely, but you can minimize it so that you can achieve a faster reading speed.

Mind Mapping and Tony Buzan

Tony Buzan's book *Speed Reading* was published in 1971, but his biggest contribution to the field was when he developed mind mapping. This was a way to take non-linear notes, which he wrote about in several other books. However, in his book about speed reading, the "Mind Map Organic Study Technique" was broken into two sections. The first was preparation. This meant you set a time for your studying, choosing how much material you were going to cover, checking to see the amount of knowledge you have already, and creating goals in the form of questions.

The second part is application. This is where you survey, preview, inview, and review. Buzan provided interesting insights into reading and the issues that normally hold back those who read slowly, but the majority of his book covers textual comprehension tests and mechanical number-spotting. He believes that you should build vocabulary and he also lists the meanings of 51 suffixes and 80 prefixes.

Non-Conscious Mind

The next big jump in speed reading history was focusing on the abilities of the non-conscious mind. Georgi Lozanov, a Bulgarian educationist, psychotherapist, and doctor, created the "Suggestology Research Institute" in Sofia, in 1966. He came up with a teaching method that he referred to as Suggestopedia where learning was made pleasurable and natural, which it reflected how children learned while also drawing on the capacity of the non-conscious mind.

When the western world took up Lozanov's approach, they referred to it as Accelerated Learning. In 1981, Norman Dixon's book *Preconscious Processing* was published. In it, he detailed his work on the brain's ability to take information in without the need for conscious awareness and how priming affected a person's behavior without their knowledge.

He came to the conclusion that words don't have to be consciously perceived for a person to recognize them. This was particularly relevant when it comes to PhotoReading techniques where a person will look quickly, around a second on each page, at each page in a book without actually reading it.

Richard Welch previously came to this conclusion. He was considered the "father of mental photography." He ran a lot of Evelyn Wood type courses to come up with Subliminal Dynamics. He made amazing claims for his system, which meant you had to eliminate subvocalization altogether. It also included a 16-year-old boy who was dyslexic, who could also take in 6,000 words a minute and still scored 90 percent on a comprehension test.

Welch believed that it wasn't necessary for a person to read material multiple times for it to sink in. He believed that the participants in his classes would take in regular information at a rate of two seconds on each page, or faster. They would even sometimes hold the book upside down because the subconscious mind knows no bounds. Even though the readers didn't feel as if they had read, the information was still able to find a way into the brain and into their subconscious.

Paul Scheele attended a Richard Welch course and came up with his own system that he called "The PhotoReading Whole Mind System," which depended on downloading. Paul named this the PhotoReading step, but his system explained that the information that had traveled directly to the non-conscious mind had to be activated for it to be useful.

His five steps were:

1. Prepare – create your purpose and get yourself in a good state.

2. Preview

3. PhotoRead – this includes going into photofocus.

4. Postview – this is similar to previewing.

5. Activate.

The biggest problem people had with this system was understanding the activation process, which was just as important as the other four steps, but which actually took around twice as much time than the other steps put together.

The activation process started with an incubation period, which meant they had to wait for at least 20 minutes, preferably overnight. This was for the mind to process things. After this, you would work with your book using super-reading, rapid reading, and mind mapping. After this, the reader would be expected to remember the book much in the same way they would with traditional reading.

This brings us pretty much to today in the speed reading world. People are developing new tools, and there are loads of apps that people have created. Figuring out which ones are helpful and which ones aren't is the hard part, but that's why you have this book.

How the Mind Works

If you are actually reading this, then you are probably an accomplished reader. The truth is, you have probably forgotten, at this point in your life, how much work you had to do before you ever learned how to read. Chances are you probably never even think about what is going on in your brain while you are reading your email or this month's book club book.

And yet, there is no other part of you that plays such an important role in learning to read than your always ready reading brain.

There's a lot of things that have to happen in order for a kid to learn to read and then to comprehend what they read, according to Nadine Gaab, Ph.D. Infants also have to learn how to process sounds. By preschool or early kindergarten, a child has to learn phonological processing, which means they have the ability to manipulate the sounds of language, like deleting or adding sounds to create words. We start developing language skills that we need for reading right when we start making gurgles as babies. The different sounds that we encounter in our environment as infants set your language acquisition skills into play. This readies the brain language-based communication, which includes reading.

Whenever a baby hears speech, their brain will learn the rules of language that will then translate to reading. Things like simple nursery rhymes are able to help a baby's brain start to create sound differentiation and to make phonemic awareness, which is an essential building block to get ready to read. Once the child is ready to read effectively, the brain has already performed a lot of tasks in coordinating sounds to language, and it is completely prepared to coordinate the language necessary for reading, and subsequently from reading to comprehension.

The child will then have to learn to read single words and then grow the vocab that is necessary to read and to understand full sentences and paragraphs. Finally, they will master the ability to read fluently at a normal speed.

As complex as reading is, thanks to neuroscience developments and technology we can target key learning spots within your brain and identify the parts and neural pathways that the brain uses when you are reading. We are not only able to understand why struggling readers struggle and strong readers read well, but we can also help all readers on their journey from early language acquisition to comprehension and reading, which is a journey that only happens in your brain.

There are a lot of brain regions involved in comprehension and reading. Among those is the temporal lobe. This is the spot responsible for phonological awareness and for discriminating and decoding sounds. Then there is the Broca's area in the frontal lobe. This is the area that governs language comprehension and speech production. Lastly, there is supramarginal and angular gyrus. These link the different areas of the brain so that the shapes of the letters can be placed together to create words.

In addition to these areas, there are also several important white-matter pathways that are needed for reading. White matter is a group of nerve fibers inside the brain. It is called white matter because of the white color of myelin, which is the fatty substance that insulates these brain fibers. These areas help the brain function and learn.

Gaab compares these tracts to highway systems that provide a connection from the back of the brain's reading network all the way to the front. For a person to comprehend and read, this highway system has to be wide enough for several pieces of information to travel at the same time. This highway also needs to be smooth. This is to make sure that the information is able to flow at a high rate of speed. This is because you never want the information to stop.

In the 2012 *Proceedings of the National Academy of Sciences*, Stanford University neuroscientists relayed that a young child's reading ability is connected to the growth of the white matter in the brain, specifically the arcuate nucleus. This is what connects the brain's language centers. It is also important for the interior longitudinal fasciculus, which is what links all of these language centers with the areas of the brain that help process visual information. They discovered that strong readers start with strong signals in both tracts, which only grow stronger through the years. The opposite also occurs for those who are weaker readers.

These white matter tracts are what become compromised in children with dyslexia. These tracts could be too narrow, bumpy, or crowded for normal comprehension and reading to happen. Even in the most fluent of readers, subtle differences in white matter can affect their reading ability.

Emerging readers are able to build up strong reading skills with focus and repetitive practice.

Bookworms are now able to rejoice in the fact that there is a way that they can speed up their reading. Some people were naturally born with an extremely long reading list, and a life's mission to finish them all from cover to cover, but they can seem daunting. The majority of people are able to read 200 to 400 words each minute. This is the average time that it takes for a person to read a word, process its phonetics inside the brain, and then picture it happening as the book moves on.

What if somebody told you that you could read up to two to three times, maybe five, times faster than you can now by just practicing? Just bringing your reading speed up to 500 words a minute can make a very big difference between taking a month to read a book to only two weeks.

Traditional reading is made so that you carry your eyes from left to right as well as the words sequentially, but during this, your eyes will naturally search for a single point in every word that could end up being the key to getting your words per minute up to 1,000.

The ORP, or optimal recognition point, is a certain place toward the middle of the word. Once your eyes are able to find the ORP, in just milliseconds the brain will start to process the whole word and the meaning. The eye will continue to follow all of the words within a sentence until it builds them up to form a complete sentence. After your eyes have found punctuation, the brain will cue itself to create a coherent thought. Then your eyes will move onto the next sentence until you have finished reading the book.

In all of those precious hours that you spend reading, a character could have fallen in and out of love, an evil king could have been overtaken by a noble knight brigade, or a scientist may have found a new cure through trial and error. No matter what genre, there are new reading comprehension tools that teenagers have started to use while in high school. Technology Chief Mail Maurer and MIT Professor Frank Waldman launched Spritz in 2013, and it has already been changed into 20 different languages that have been used in 50 countries. Penn Schoen Berland, a statistical research group, administered the Spritz comprehension test to 1000 readers from different age groups. They improved their reading speed by an average of 40%.

The brain takes around 80% of its time trying to find the ORP and the rest of the time it works on comprehending the word. The eye can only process around a dozen characters at any given time. Spritz streamlines the words to the reader through a video with the ORP highlighted by the color red. This means that the eye won't have to reposition itself and waste time searching. Getting rid of the need for the eye to move is the secret weapon of this piece of technology.

The Brain's Language Processing Process

While some of this may seem like I am telling you speed reading is wrong, and you shouldn't do it, I'm not. I'm telling you this so that you can get to know both sides of the story, and so that you can fully understand the way the brain works.

Contrary to what you may have thought, reading isn't natural, and it never has been. An estimated 150,000 to 50,000 years ago, humans invented language, but archaeological researchers haven't been able to figure out when it completely emerged into our communication toolbox. The alphabet itself is just four to five thousand years old, and more than likely enough time hasn't passed for specialized areas of the human brain to evolve into reading-friendly machines, at least according to an Oxford University research team.

The major drawback to making our brains adapt to a new reading strategy is very similar to having to teach a new dog, new tricks. The ABCs we know haven't been around for a long enough time for scientists to look at our mastery of them. When we are developing new skills, the connective nerve in the brain will make new highways to move around this information. This will constantly make us more efficient, adept, and better at a certain skill. When you switch to an ORP-focused form of reading, you could end up losing some of the strength in the muscles of the brain that the human race has developed over the last thousand years or so.

Back in 2009, Georgetown University Medical Center found the important word-processing brain cells were located at the left side of the brain. The senior author of the study, Dr. Maximilian Riesenhuber, explained that reading relies on neural representations that are dependent on experience. He also explained that evolution never provided us with little dictionaries inside of the mind.

With time, humans were able to collect words and add them to their brain's dictionary database. We then memorized these words and processed their meanings through our left visual cortex. This is where written words are changed into complete units that represent neighbors, dogs, siblings, trees, and emotions. When you translate these little black lines and squiggles, they move throughout the eyes, into the flesh walls at the back of your optic nerve. At this point, the messages are then sent to, translated, and changed into ideas, concepts, visuals, messages, and stories.

For all you bibliophiles out there, read on. Engage those neurons and make them turn on the speech motor parts of your brain while all of those images flood into the mid and engage the fluidity of sounds and symbols into full words and meanings.

Why Your Brain Needs to Read

Reading makes your brain work. Reading works your mind much like exercise works your body. It gives you a chance to roam through the expanses of history, space, time and offers you a deeper view of emotions, concepts, ideas, and knowledge.

Your brain on books is active. It is making new connections, changing, growing, and making different patterns, depending on what you choose to read.

Reading helps to improve your brain's connectivity. The brain will change and develop in very fascinating ways when you read.

As you are reading these words, your brain is working to decode a series of abstract symbols and synthesize what results come up into complex ideas. It is a very amazing process.

You can liken the collaborative work of the brain to a symphony orchestra with all of the various areas of the brain working with each other, just like sections of instruments, to improve our brain's ability to change the written text that is in front of us.

Reading also works to rewire the brain. The author, Maryanne Wolf, explains this in her book, *Proust and the Squad: The Story and Science of the Reading Brain*. Basically, humans invented reading a few thousand years ago. When we invented this, we changed the way the brain works, which made the way we think expand. This, in turn, altered our intellectual evolution. Our ancestors' creation was only able to happen because of the amazing abilities of the brain to make these new connections among all of its existing structures.

Reading involves many different brain functions, which include auditory and visual process, comprehension, fluency, phonemic awareness, and more. The same parts of the brain that are stimulated by experiencing something are also stimulated through reading.

Research has found that reading can not only help with fluid intelligence, but it can also help with emotional intelligence as well as reading comprehension. Fluid intelligence is your ability to solve problems, find important patterns, and understand things.

Reading is also able to increase your fluid intelligence, and this increase in fluid intelligence will also help improve your reading comprehension. Stanford research has found neurological differences between focused reading and reading for pleasure. The blood flow to neural areas was different depending on how you conduct your reading.

When it comes to fiction, it is a social experience. This type of reading plays a very important role in social function. When you are reading fiction, you will mentally imagine what is happening, the characters, the situation, and the details that are being described. It's an immersion process.

Emory University researchers found that fiction improves the connections in the areas of the brain that handle language reception. Gregory Berns, the lead neuroscientist, and author said that it is also able to wire into processes that are called grounded cognition.

During a 30 minute span of time, the average human will split their time between constantly reacting to notifications, checking their social media, talking to co-workers, checking their email, and working on a task.

Reading will not only improve the connectivity of the brain, but it will also improve the attention spans, concentration, and focus. If you have a hard time focusing, start reading more and it will improve your attention span.

When you are reading, your attention is completely focused on that story or it is gaining knowledge about a certain subject. All of the world around you will just fall away, and you are able to immerse yourself in that text to absorb the material.

Books that have structure will encourage you to think in a certain sequence. The more you read, the more the brain will link your cause and effect. It's a good idea to try reading for 15 to 20 minutes each morning before you go to work. If you take public transportation, you can read on your commute. You will be amazed at how more focused you are when you make your way to the office.

Speed Reading Mindset

In order to be successful at speed reading, it will require you to embrace and understand certain qualities of your mind. Because of all the extremely different approaches and all of the needed behaviors, the unprepared learner may end up giving up. Instead of allowing you to succumb to this premature emotional response, succeeding in speed reading requires that you appreciate the natural reaction that your mind will have to different and new ways of acting, and do something about it.

The human mind is pretty good at wanting to resist a lot of change; especially if it means that it is going to take any extra conscious effort. This conscious effort will require more energy than the unconscious mind wants to give.

How this works for somebody who is just learning to speed read goes a little like this:

They start out being excited about the chance to achieve their outcome to easily read multiple times than their usual speed. They start to learn a couple of different techniques. These techniques are all radically different than the multiple years of reading they already have. They start to become frustrated. They may try out some of these techniques again, but they still struggle. Then their mind makes a conclusion, "I can't do this."Or, they may even think, "This doesn't work."

They could also experience some other negative self-talk experiences. The point here is that they are allowing themselves to yield to that area of their mind that is resistant to change. So they stop practicing.

In the end, nothing changes.

You can't let this happen to you. You have to understand that disciplining your mind's reaction to this process of change is important to your outcome.

In the book *Society of Mind*, Marvin Minky talks about the "anti-joy of learning." He explains that during the early stages of acquiring new skills a person will have to adopt a little bit of an anti-pleasure attitude. This means that when you start to become frustrated and not all that successful you may want to tell yourself, "Good this has given me the chance to experience some awkwardness and make some new mistakes!"

Think about the last thing I just wrote. Do you enjoy experiencing mistakes and awkwardness? A lot of people try to avoid these types of situations. However, the best learners embrace these moments of awkwardness and mistakes because they understand that it is the path to eventual mastery. There are areas of the mind that feel this is horrible while there are other areas that enjoy forcing those first parts to work. Anybody who has managed to achieve a large amount of growth knows and appreciates these feelings of anti-joy. Any skill that is worthwhile is going to require this type of mental mindset.

What about you? Are you going to be able to embrace this feeling of anti-joy in the learning process so that you can master speed reading? Without embracing this you are not going to succeed and you will probably be bombarded with a bunch of information that you have to digest to be successful in the future.

Getting Ready to Read

It's important that you get yourself ready before you start to read so that your mindset is right. In most things that we do, we prepare for things in some fashion. Players and athletes warm up and stretch before they play a game. Drivers let their cars warm up, especially when it's cold. Farmer's prep the field before they plant. But most students will hardly ever think of warming up or preparing before they start to read. Students are just expected to go from lit class to math class to geography without doing anything to get their brains to switch gears.

You will discover that you will be more efficient at reading when you take the time to get ready before you start to read. Students that allow themselves to prepare to read will end up remembering more of the things that they read, are able to concentrate more fully, and to make better connections between ideas.

Learning in schools is made up of 85% text, so it's important that you are able to find the information that is within that text. How can you prepare to read?

- State your purpose

- Fix where your point of attention is going to be and enter the best state of mind.

Before you start reading, why are you reading? If you say: because I need to answer some questions about the text, you are probably not going to remember what you are reading or you won't retain the things you read. You will notice that you are just flipping through your book without a point, and you will end up wasting your time.

"If you are not going anywhere, any road will take you there." – West African Proverb

Experts in reading have found six fundamental purposes for reading:

1. To be entertained.

2. To apply the things you have read.

3. To evaluate what you read.

4. To answer certain questions.

5. To discover important details.

6. To grasp a message.

Keep in mind that reading with purpose is your first step towards remembering and understanding what you have read.

Now, I want you to really ask yourself, "Why am I reading this? What is the purpose? What is it that I am expecting to be able to know or do because of your reading?" You have to think about your reading in terms of outcomes.

- I am trying to find concrete figures and facts.

- I want several different opinions on a certain topic.

- I want to be able to completely answer questions about the topic.

- I want to know what is going to happen next.

- I want to get evidence to support my argument.

- I want to get a good idea or a broad overview of a topic.

- I want to completely learn the topic and commit it to memory.

Your purpose will define your method of reading.

There are mainly three basic types of reading we all do:

1. Pleasure reading: when you are reading only for pleasure or to really appreciate an author's ability and style.

2. Critical reading: to find concepts and ideas that need a thorough analysis.

3. Quick reference reading: when you are looking for certain information to answer your questions or a certain question.

The best readers will always match their method to their purpose. So you have to be completely clear about your reason for reading right from the start.

There is another big reason why you need to state your purpose. Reading experts agree that active readers are the best readers. To read actively means a lot of things. Far too often people will read mindlessly, hoping that the important information will just sink in somehow and it will then eventually surface at some point when they need it.

In a sense, when you set a purpose you will be choosing a reading process. The process or purpose that you pick will change how you encounter your text. For example, if you were going to read the newspaper, you will probably not want to read this the same way you would a textbook.

Once you have figured out your purpose for reading, you can start your reading process. All of this works together with the different speed reading techniques you will learn in this book. This will ensure that your comprehension of the text doesn't fail, and it will make sure that you can get the most from what you are reading. There may be times, though, when you are deciding on your purpose for reading that you find that you don't feel the need to speed read, and that is perfectly okay as well.

How Speed Reading Works

"I cannot remember the books I've read any more than the meals I have eaten; even so, they have made me." – Ralph Waldo Emerson

Chances are if you are reading this book, you are interested in reading more books in a shorter amount of time without losing any of your comprehension. Well, I'm going to present to you a quick explanation and technique for speed reading. The great thing for you is that all you are going to need is an e-reader, computer, or smartphone and a simple adjustment. Before we dive into this method, let's quickly glance over two common speed reading techniques, which will be covered more in-depth in a later chapter.

Conventional Strategies

Most speed reading techniques will train you to get rid of subvocalization and chunking works into groups. Basically, this means that you suppress your urge to vocalize what you are reading in your mind so that you are able to interpret the words as symbols or pictures.

The theory is that if you get super good at this you will end up turning entire paragraphs into symbols instead of just single words. The sentence "The man walked down the street and bumped into a green lamppost" isn't read by individual words, but is instantly seen as a single image in your mind.

Some people find this idea hard to grasp. This is mainly because the spoken language has existed a lot longer than written language. Not only does this cause your body to go evolutionarily backward, so that makes it almost impossible to completely get rid of your subvocalizing.

In even the best speed readers, subvocalization can be detected in their vocal chords. The second problem that people have with this technique is that readers will normally chunk naturally. Very rarely do people sound out every the, and, a, when and they will simply describe things like a black cat, which are easy to picture.

Thirdly, people will often find it harder to comprehend what they read when they don't subvocalize. A lot of experts like to describe that speed reading is only a methodical way of skimming. While this isn't completely true, it is important to find the speed reading strategy that works best for you.

It's also important to remember that there is a time and place to speed read. It is extremely useful when you want to skim through academic papers and articles so that you can find all the bits of information that you need.

When it comes to writers, speed reading can be a very bad idea. They need to take in language just like it is expressed, and everybody has to subvocalize when they are writing. Speed reading through literature is a lot like watching amazing TV at two times the speed, which I will talk about later on in the book.

PhotoReading

This is a fairly new technique for speed reading, and it is easy to do. But that's not why I have placed it early on in the book. The only thing you have to do is to flick through your book while looking rapidly down the middle of the pages. This will give your unconscious mind time to absorb the information that you need in order to recall the information at a later time.

PhotoReading gives you the chance to take in 25,000 words a minute, or as many of the PhotoReading enthusiast like to say "The speed at which our brains think." Keep in mind though, if something sounds too good to be true, it typically is.

The crazy smart people at NASA performed a very in-depth study on the art of PhotoReading and came to the conclusion that:

"These results clearly indicate that there is no benefit to using the PhotoReading technique. The extremely rapid reading rates claimed by PhotoReaders were not observed; indeed the reading rates were generally comparable to those for normal reading."

Steve Pavlina and Paul Scheele, well known personal-development gurus, have been big fans of this form of speed reading, but they probably have other motives. But that's not the point of this book. If you find it helpful and it works for you, then so be it.

Speed Reading, No Gimmicks

You can read a lot faster without having to focus on just the conventional speed reading methods, and without the need of outrageous course fees. That's not to say you shouldn't also try and use the techniques that we cover later on. This first method that I am going to cover with you is a science-based method and you can use it instantly without training.

This method hasn't been talked about much that I know of. There is an academic article that talked about a study on this particular technique called *How Physical Text Layout Affects Reading From the Screen* written by Mary C. Dyson. She explained that the Kolers et al. (1981) study found that smaller characters, where there were more characters on every line, were read at a faster rate. The full screen and two-thirds widths were read faster than the one-third screen widths were. When you combine the two densities, positive things happen that indicate that when there are more characters on each line, the person can read at a faster rate.

Now, the downside of this is that you have to be reading on a tablet, e-reader, computer, or phone. On those devices, you can typically adjust the size of the text, but you can't do that with hard copies of books. That means this won't work every time you read.

According to Dyson, the best line length for the best reading speed is 100 characters per line. For this example, we will assume that you are using an Amazon Kindle. For other devices, you will have to play around to see how to change the text size. On your Kindle, click "Aa Tab" and then change the settings to the second to smallest text size.

At this setting, if you hold the device horizontally, the characters per line will come out to around 80. If you go to the smallest setting, you will probably be straining your eyes too much to read it.

For newer versions of the Kindle and other e-reading devices, you can use the settings above as a guide. You will want to play around to see which size comes out to around 80 to 100 characters per line. Yes, this means you will have to count the letters in the line of text, but once you have found the best setting, you won't have to do that again.

Now, this speed reading hack won't necessarily put you at reading quadruple your normal reading speed like PhotoReading ads typically promised, but if you constantly use this method, over a period of time it will give your reading abilities a dramatic effect.

Even if you only notice that your reading speed for a single book has been reduced by 45 to 90 minutes that means that you could still fit in an extra ten to 20 books each year. The great thing is that this technique doesn't even require you to do anything different.

That's it for your first technique. Continue reading to learn more techniques for speed reading that works for any format and not just e-readers.

Correct Application for Reading

Having the ability to join the sounds of different letters together to correctly sound out an entire word doesn't mean that you are a good reader. True reading consists of a lot of other things. This includes understanding what you are reading and creating your own opinions about the things that you are reading. Buzan broke this process down into several different phases, and they all have to be worked on in order to supercharge your reading skills.

1. Recognition – This is the basic knowledge of alphabetic symbols.

2. Assimilation – This is the actual physical process where the light is reflected by the word, the eye receives it, and then it is transferred through your optic nerve into the brain.

3. Intra-integration – This is your basic understanding. You achieve this by

connecting the different areas of the information.

4. Extra-integration – This is where you connect all of your previously gained information to the new information that you have learned.

5. Retain – This is where you retain the information.

6. Remember – This is your ability to access all of the information that you have stored away.

7. Communication – This is being able to share the information you have stored by means of visualizing, writing, and talking. But you can also do this step by just thinking about the information. This means that you share it with yourself just inside your mind.

Misunderstandings about Reading

Everybody assumes that once a child is able to read through a book in silence that they have learned how to read. But this is about the same as learning how to drive a sports car and the driving along the road in a lawnmower. This would mean that any more development in the skill of reading is only going to be small, especially if they are only doing day-to-day reading, which is the kind that will take place out of school and college environments.

It's just like learning, over time, how to take the corners on the road just a little bit quicker in the lawnmower. Now, maybe, in the end, the kid will end up getting to a speed of 200 words per minutes. The majority of grown-ups that continue with the lawnmower method will only make it to 250 words per minute. A college student may be able to push themselves with their strong willpower and coffee up to 400 words per minute. Bu this still only puts them in a car with an engine that is only slightly faster than that tired old lawnmower. With not much effort, a person can hit the 1000 words per minute mark, and then your next stop is Formula One or NASCAR.

A lot of you reading this may get to this point and be like, "Hey, surely all of this speeding up will cause me to lower my understanding of the text." That's not true. It takes a lot of energy to consume things from syllable, to word, to sentence, and then to the complete message. That is why Evelyn Wood believed that an average person is able to think about around 5000 words per minute. But, this same person is probably only driving that same old lawnmower and reading at speed of 250 words per minute. The reason for this is because a lot of students will get frustrated and bored while they are reading. This is because they think at a faster speed than they read. Moreover, the majority of texts will contain a lot of wasted words; so that means you have a lot of stuff that you shouldn't even have to process. The message will probably be a lot clearer once you get rid of that stuff.

Here's a fun fact for you. Did you realize that people have only recently learned how to read things in silence? This means that before this time they were only able to read things out loud. Could you imagine walking into a library where everybody is just screaming so that they can hear what they are reading to themselves over everybody else?

The Benefits of Speed Reading

To me, speed reading isn't just about being able to read faster. The goals most people have are being able to comprehend the information better and to retain that information a little longer. They want the entire package.

Trying to decide if you are going to learn how to speed read or not isn't easy and it's important to know all of the good and bad things about it. When you are speed reading you will be able to finish more books, which means that you will stay ahead on your reading list. Even if you only use the skimming method, you will still be able to understand the essentials of the books that you will speed read through. Additionally, you will also be the envy of your book club.

Another great thing that comes along with speed reading is that with the increase of books you are reading, the more recommendations you will be able to make. It will also give you the chance to make it through books that are outside of your comfort zone because you will have more time and more desire to enrich your knowledge.

Even if you can't completely see it, speed reading will also make a difference in your budget. Picture yourself heading to the library and scanning through the first few chapters. You will definitely be able to figure out if you are going to like the book enough to buy it. You will also find that you have more time for other hobbies that you enjoy since you will be speed reading through your books. You will also have time for those less-fun chores that you have to do.

If you like reading on the train or bus, you might find it hard to isolate yourself from the things going on around you. When you speed read, you will find that it becomes easier for you to concentrate. Another great thing is that you don't have to have anything fancy with you in order to speed read. As low tech as it may seem, all you need is a pointer finger, and you can do this no matter where you are.

But, let's not forget about the fact that there are speed reading tools that you can download and use wherever you are. This means you have even more chances to use technology. With these devices, you will sometimes have the chance to input your text into the device, and you can practice speed reading your stories.

A lot of people like the idea of speed reading, especially when it comes to research. This is because you can quickly skim through text and focus on finding the things that you are searching for. You will then focus your reading on the parts of the text that you need to instead of all the other stuff that won't do you any good.

Speed reading provides you with a large number of benefits for everybody in their day-to-day life, especially when it comes to students, business people, and for anybody that likes to read a lot.

With so much information zooming at us every single day, investing some time in learning speed reading strategies just makes sense. Just picture yourself zipping through emails at double the time you normally do or whipping through all of the social media updates posted by your friends and responding to them quickly.

However, since most speed reading strategies will take a little time for you to learn and you already have a busy life, you are probably thinking why you should add another item to your to-do list. Let's go through some of the several benefits that speed reading will bring you.

Improved Memory

As you know, the brain works like a muscle. If we work to train our brains, it will continue to grow stronger and it will be able to work more efficiently. Speed reading will make you challenge your brain so that it performs at a higher level. When you are training your brain to take in information at a faster pace, other parts of your brain will also start to improve, like your memory. Memory, when reading, works like a stabilizer muscle, which gets a lot of work when you are speed reading.

This improved memory will also move into other areas of your life. Since memory also plays a big part in creativity, you will also notice that you will become more creative in all things you do.

Relaxation

Reading is a super relaxing pastime, and this is true for any speed that you read at. This means that it can help you to reduce your stress because it gets rid of your thoughts about all of your burdens and worries. Indeed, if you have the right book, it can make all of those negative thoughts in your head disappear. Your mood can change instantly. When you are able to read faster, you will get more fully absorbed in the material. Speed reading is able to help shut you off from the world around you and to allow you to really lose yourself in the book that you are reading. Try to add more reading into your life for just one month you will see the difference.

Sophistication: Your Thinking Ability Will Improve

Speed reading affects your brain's neuroplasticity. This means that your brain will be able to make new connections. This means not only will you notice an improvement in your creativity, but your thinking will improve as well.

Better Focus

Do you find that you have problems focusing on tasks? Speed reading skills have the ability to help you focus on things as well. You will notice that you are more interested in the things that you read, and with the mixture of your enhanced creativity, you will start to notice that you become more eager to extend your education.

The majority of people read around 200 words each minute, but there are others that can read up to 300 words each minute. Why is there such a large gap between these? There are two main reasons why. The first is that the traditional style of reading that we are all taught is not all that efficient. The second is because we lack focus. People that aren't focused when they are reading allow their minds to wander and then thoughts will start to pop up. Speed reading will help to build up that focus.

Information is constantly running at us in a million different directions. A lot of people will try to multi-task to try and get more things done. This will only lead to a more fragmented attention. This just leads to overall inefficiency.

Better Ambition: You Will Find That You Are More Inspired

When you have better-thinking abilities, fresh creativity, better memory, as well as the ability to focus on what you are working on, you will discover that you are more ambitious when it comes to your career. You will find your world expands. You will become eager and ready to fight your way to the top of the career ladder within your chosen career field.

Higher Levels of Self-Confidence

Currently, how comfortable are you when it comes to talking to your boss? If you fully understand your company and the competitors, the marketplace, and the financial news, you will start to feel more confident that you will be able to handle all of their questions. You will start to make confident suggestions to your department as well as the entire business.

I think that this happens because you know that you are able to learn just about any aspect of life faster after you have created the ability to comprehend more and read faster. Once you have been able to improve your ability to learn and read faster, you will start to find more and more doors that are open for you so that you can get more options. The reason for this is that every article or book, whether it's nonfiction or fiction, helps us to change our awareness and then we will start to see more depth in our lives. The depth that you develop will boost your self-confidence.

Think about being able to put your point of view across to a person that you know is only going to disagree with you? Would you be comfortable in doing that? In all of these situations, you will notice that you feel more at ease from being well-read.

Improved Logic

Your brain is exercised when you read. When you work to train your brain to read things faster, something amazing will happen. The brain will then become more efficient at sorting through information and discovering correlations with other pieces of information that you previously had. The better your reading speed becomes, the quicker this process happens, you will start to automatically notice improvements in your logic as you start to get more used to responding quicker to what used to take you a lot longer to process. After you have learned how to speed read, you will find yourself doing better at games of logic, such as chess. These skills will also make their way into all of your everyday problem-solving.

Emotional Well-being

In general, reading tends to be relaxing. Reading is able to help you reduce your stress because it will take your mind off of your worries and other issues that aren't beneficial or healthy. When you learn to read faster, you will notice that you become more absorbed in the material. This will make you focus mainly on the information that you are reading through. This is what is called active-meditation. Active-meditation is a state of meditation that you achieve by doing a certain activity. In this state you are able to release a lot of tension and up your emotional well-being.

Reduces Fatigue

A person who reads quickly will likely not experience as much fatigue as a person who reads slower because of the extended time and concentration that it will take for them to read the same length of text. Learning how to speed read is a pretty good skill to learn early in your life so that you can prevent eye strain as well as any other eye problems.

Empowerment: You Feel Comfortable Wherever You Are

There will always be people who are judging you, every day, with every word that you speak. When you are sitting in a business meeting, you will often hesitate to share your point of view if you aren't completely sure of the facts. Reading, as well as comprehending the things you have read, will give you fast facts so that you can turn into knowledge.

When you are in social situations, you are more comfortable with your friends. They all know you. However, when you are at parties, you have to talk about things. And when other people are talking about different topics, you will want to have an opinion. Speed reading through the news, from gossip to world events, will give you a lot of things to keep conversations going.

Thought Leadership

All thought leaders in all fields are innovative. The reason they are innovative is that they use the things they know. They will cross-pollinate their ideas. Tina Seelig explained that being able to combine and connect ideas that aren't so obvious and objects that are important for innovation is an important part of the creative-thinking process. With your ability to be able to reframe different problems, it will make use of your imagination and this will then unlock the innovation engine in your mind. Being able to speed reading could end up leading you all the way to the next billion-dollar idea, and the chance to implement that said idea.

Money: You Will Have Better Employment Access

Money means you will have security and freedom for you and your family. Whether you are looking to get a promotion at work, or you want to get a better job. Knowledge is the best way to do so. If you are looking to get a promotion, you have to stand out amongst the others. Formal advanced education and online courses help you to do just that. When you have a degree, it will make you look more attractive to your possible employers in general. Equally, when you have obtained a degree or certification that your competition doesn't have will increase your value. With the increased value, it will translate into more income. Speed reading will help you to better your education. You will be able to easily manage all of the coursework for your classes.

Better Problem Solving Skills

Everybody will be faced with some challenges. Your subconscious mind is able to figure these things out. Speed reading gives your mind the ability to stream more of that information to your subconscious mind. When you have more information, your subconscious will be able to figure out your problems.

These are just a few of the benefits that come along with learning how to speed read.

Downsides

While speed reading will provide you with a lot of benefits, and, overall, it is a great skill to have, it's important that you know the downsides that it can bring.

My views of the disadvantages of speed reading may not mean the same thing to you, so that means it is important that you realize you have the final say when it comes to whether you choose to learn how to speed read or not.

An interesting thing when it comes to speed reading if you are just a beginner or even extremely experienced, the risk of skimming through your text and not actually reading anything is very high. The odds are you will end up skipping some important details, especially if you do enjoy reading the twists in books.

When you skim through your reading, you could end up missing out on the best parts of your books. This means you won't be able to share all of the same emotions that all of the other readers do. Other people could end up talking about an interesting section that you ended up missing, and then you would be in an awkward position. You won't be able to say anything or input any other important information.

For most people, speed reading is all about going through the pages with only your eyes and then extracting the parts that mean the most to them. This relates a lot to getting a basic idea of what the text is actually about. This is the reason why you may end up missing some of the most important, but hidden information.

If you enjoy reading science fiction novels, then speed reading probably isn't going to be a good idea since you will probably miss out on some of the subtler details. Let's not forget when an author exaggerates certain details and this may end up appearing pretty interesting while you are skimming through the text and may make you think that the theme is something completely different than what it actually is.

Speed reading is a fun thing to do, but it is pretty hard to look away and then still remain on track. It's hard for a person to look away from their text and then come back to it at the same spot when they are speed reading, which can make it a lot harder to understand when you are reading.

When Not to Speed Read

While speed reading is a wonderful skill to have, there are times when you shouldn't speed read, or at least you want to. Everything I'm going to cover in this chapter is subjective and you can make your own decision with the information I give you. The most important thing that you need to remember is that if you are going to have to reiterate any information in the text to somebody else, you may want to slow down your reading so that you can highlight and take notes.

Literature

Harold Bloom, a celebrated academic, is a speed reader. In a blink of an eye, he has probably turned the page, likely twice. In his prime, he was able to read 1,000 pages in an hour, which means that he would be able to get through *Jane Eyre* during lunch, and he would have still had time to make it through half of *Ulysses* before heading back to class. I can't speak for you, but that makes me feel like I am a slack-jawed, slow simian whose frontal-lobe is lacking.

The average reader creeps their way through prose at around 250 to 300 words a minute, which comes out to around a page a minute. Bloom was cut from a rare cloth because he is able to whip through around 16 pages every minute and he can still remember nearly everything he reads. It's not that easy for the rest of the human race.

When it comes to people who participate in the World Championship Speed Reading Competition, the best participants will read 1,000 to 2,000 words a minute, but they typically only retain 50%. This isn't all that great when you read literature. What would be the point of reading a book when you can only remember half of it once you're done?

So why would people want to speed read literature? The simple answer would be so that they can boast about how many books they have read. Think about it, did the world's great novelists really spend most of their lives agonizing over the rhythm and pitch of their books so that some post-modern reader that is looking to be time-efficient could skim over? I think not.

Speed reading is a decent tool for love letters, textbooks, and office documents, but for prose, it should be savored. The biggest joy that comes from reading prose is hearing our mind pronounce the words, and to imagine the speech.

If you don't believe me, here is an example. The first is the full text and the second is the skimmed version.

"It was the best of times, it was the worst of times, it was the age of wisdom, it was the age of foolishness, it was the epoch of belief, it was the epoch of incredulity, it was the season of Light, it

was the season of Darkness, it was the spring of hope, it was the winter of despair." – Charles Dickens, A Tale of Two Cities (1859)

"Best times/worst times, age wisdom/foolishness, epoch belief/incredulity, season Light/Darkness, spring hope, winter, despair." – Charles Dickens, the skimmed version.

Which version would you rather read? You can't appreciate the nuances of the writing if you only skim through it.

When You Are Stressed

This may sound odd, but reading at a regular pace is able to help you reduce stress. That means if you are feeling rather stressed out, go at a regular pace instead of a fast pace.

When you read slowly, you will be able to engage more with the book, and it also means that you will put away your social media and phone, which also negatively affects your attention span. This will force your mind to focus on a single item at a time, which will work to keep you from being bombarded by the world around you.

When You Need to Make Knowledgeable Connections

A big advantage of reading at an average pace is that you will be able to absorb the new information in the text and to make connections with other information you know. When you allow the brain to absorb things more slowly, the facts in what you are reading, no matter what it is, you will find it easier to connect to your "web of knowledge."

This is full of stories, memories, ideas, and other facts that you have already learned. This will help you to make valuable associations between things you have already learned and new things that you are learning. This is especially important when you are going to have to teach the information to somebody else.

Testing Your Speed

When you are learning how to speed read you have to keep a record of your progress. When you monitor your reading speed as you are training, it will help you to observe all of your advances, and, when you don't observe any, figure out where your problem is and fix it. Hence, you have to know what your reading speed is.

Measuring Three Things

When you are measuring your reading speed, it is important that you look at three different measurements. All three of these are required to completely understand how you are progressing with your reading speed.

1. Average Speed

The first thing you need to measure is your average speed. The average speed looks at the number of works that you are able to read in a single minute, even if you don't completely understand or memorize any of the information that you just read.

In order to measure your average speed, pick a page form your favorite book and then count how many words are on the page. Then you will need to take a timer to see how long it takes for you to read the entire page. Once you get done, divide the number of words on the page with the minutes it took you to read it. This is your words per minute average speed.

2. Processing Speed

When you are figuring up your reading speed, any good measurement will take into account your comprehension of what you have read, which you measure with your processing speed. The main goal of speed reading is to be able to read fast, but you also want to be able to understand the things that you have read. Hence, you will want to read fast, but you need to try to understand what it is you are reading. In order for you to figure out how much of the text you were able to understand, you need to answer a few questions once you have measured your average speed. The main problem with this, especially if you are doing this on your own and not using a website, is that you will have to ask somebody else to write these questions for you. The number of questions that you are able to correctly answer will give you your percentage of understanding.

For example, let's say that you were able to answer seven out of 12 questions correctly. You would then figure out your processing speed by:

7 * 100/12 = 58%

That means your processing speed is only 58%.

3. Memorizing Speed

The memorizing speed is how many words you are able to read and comprehend each minute. You can get this number by multiplying your average speed with your processing speed, in percentage. This means that if your average speed was 600 words per minute, and your processing speed is 75%, you would figure out your memorizing speed by:

600 * .75 = 450

As you can probably figure out, the main goal of speed reading to get you to a very high memorizing speed. In order to get that, you need to have a fast average speed and you also need to have a good processing speed.

After you have figured out your reading speed, you will probably want to figure out how good or bad that speed really is. I would recommend that you don't focus on the comparison. I believe that focusing on your progress is more important than comparing yourself to others. However, there are a lot of people who will still want that information. That is why I have provided you with that information in this chapter. The following table describes how all of the different reading speeds compare to one another.

- 1 – 100 words per minute

  o Children that are learning to read will be in this reading speed range. If a learner is not able to progress beyond this range, their reading ability is seen to be at the borderline literacy range. A reader that is in this range will more than likely not have a lot of understanding and memory of the things they have read. Reading takes a lot of work when the words per minute are below 100.

- 100 – 200 words per minute

  o A person that is within this range for reading speed is typically a person who has done the minimum amount of reading that they had to in order to make it through life. This type of person normally doesn't see reading as fun, entertaining, or relaxing. Within this reading speed range, it is pretty much impossible to stay up to date on technology, world events, and so on. The reader's memory and understanding is normally less than half of what their eyes actually see.

- 200 – 250 words per minute

  o This is what is considered to be the average range for reading speed. Without any help, most of these readers are going to be stuck in this range for the rest of their reading lives. These people are constantly slowed down through regressions, concentration problems, and reading sub-vocalization. Typically, they will understand around half of what they read.

  o

- 250 – 350 words per minute

  o The speeds in this range are just a little more than average of the majority of readers. Typically, post-high school graduates or people who are casual keen readers are in this range. These readers will normally still suffer from regressions, but they don't subvocalize as many of the words. Normally, the readers in this section end up comprehending over half of the things they read.

- 350 – 500 words per minute

  o People who score in this range for reading speed are well over the average speed. As a result, their understanding and comprehension are typically very good, around 50 to 75 percent. These people are normally avid readers and enjoy it immensely. They may still suffer from some sub-vocalization and regressions. This is mainly because their mind will still drift away.

- 500 – 800 words per minute

  - This, for speed readers, is a useful and respectable reading speed. In this area, the reader will have amazing comprehension, around 75 percent or more. They will be the types of people that enjoy reading and find it pleasurable and they have great control over their office and daily reading needs. They are the types of people who find the book better than the movie.

- 800 – 1000 words per minute

  - This is an amazingly efficient speed for reading. This is verging on what is known as power-reading. This type of reader has very little sub-vocalization and they typically don't regress at all. They are able to understand and recognize most of the words. They are normally able to understand everything that they read. They aren't pressured when they read, and they don't have reading time problems. This person is likely to be at the top of the class or a high business achiever. A person who reads at this speed is normally a person who has undergone some quality reading improvement program.

- 1000 words per minute and more

  o Now, this is an amazing feat. This person is either a tutored or natural speed reader. The readers who read at this speed are able to comprehend most everything that they read. This person has complete control over all of their needs as a reader. Reading takes up a big chunk of their life. These people normally enjoy two or more novels every week.

With this chart, we are talking only about reading and not talking about skimming. That is why reading speeds over 1300 words per minute are not possible.

Measuring with a Program

Now, I have gone through how you can measure your reading speed naturally, on your own. However, there are a lot of programs out there that can perform these calculations for you, and will already have all of the questions ready to figure out your processing speed. The following are the most popular:

- Speed Reading test online by readingsoft.com. This is a web app that will provide you with a reading test as well as comprehension questions. However, this can only be used one time because they use the same text every time.

- Free Speed Reading Test, by AceReader. This is another web app that has several different tests that come with questionnaires.

- My read speed is another web app that measures your words per minute. It has ten different tests, but it does not give you any questions to answer to get your comprehension score.

- Speed reading test, Stapes. This is one of the best web apps to find out what your reading speed is. They have several different texts to test you on, and they come with questionnaires. The fun thing about this test is that once you have finished the text it will give you some numbers for how long it would take you to make your way through some famous books based on your numbers.

There are also a lot of apps out there for tablets or smartphones that will allow you to test your reading speed. The following two are pretty good:

- Acceleread Speed Reading Trainer, by BananaBox Inc. This is the best program when you want to learn about speed reading, and to figure out your reading speed and to keep things up to date on your progress. This comes along with questionnaires for your comprehension test.

- QuickReader – eBook Reader with Speed Reading, by Inkstone Software Inc. This is a great app to speed read your books with, and it is also useful for measuring your reading speed from time to time. This app does not come with a questionnaire to test your comprehension.

When you start training yourself to speed read, it is important that you test your reading speed every two weeks so that you can observe your progress or lack thereof. If you are training properly, you should start to see an increase in your memorizing speed. If you aren't, there is probably a problem with the way that you are training and you need to make efforts to change it.

Comprehension

Sing happy tree walk blue banana apple. I'm sure you could read every word in that sentence and you understood exactly what they meant. When you sing, it makes you happy. You can walk around a tree. Blue might be your favorite color. When you take the time to look at the whole sentence, did it make sense? Absolutely, not. This sentence is nothing but nonsense. It shows the difference between the ability to read only words and understanding what we read. As veteran readers, we take this for granted because the act of reading and understanding happens at the same time. For learning readers, this relationship is clear. It is needed to become capable, strong readers.

What is Comprehension?

A simple definition for reading comprehension is the understanding of what you are reading. The definition is simple but it isn't simple to practice, learn, or teach. It is an interactive, active, and intentional process that happens before, during, and after the reader reads something in particular.

Reading comprehension is the main pillar in the act of reading. When we read a passage, we engage in a series of cognitive processes. We are using awareness and understanding of phonemes simultaneously. Phonemes are the individual pieces of sound in language. We also use phonics which is the connection and relationship between sounds, letters, and words. By using these abilities to construct or comprehend meanings from what we read. Lastly, the act of reading is how well we comprehend what we read. It can't happen independently of the other elements in this process. It is the most important and difficult of all of them.

The two elements that create the process of reading comprehension are text comprehension and vocabulary knowledge. To be able to understand what you read, you have to be able to understand vocabulary that is used in writing. If words don't make sense, then the complete story isn't going to make sense either. Children are able to draw on prior knowledge of their vocabulary. They need to constantly learn new words. The best instruction happens when they need it. Teachers and parents need to pre-teach new words that children might encounter in a book to help them understand words they aren't familiar with. To be able to understand every word they read, they need the ability to put words together to create an idea of what it says. This is called text comprehension. This is more varied and complex than vocabulary knowledge. Readers can use various comprehension methods to create a reading comprehension. These might include looking to understand, creating and answering questions, being aware and summarizing, and using the text's structure to help comprehend what is read.

How to develop comprehension?

Reading comprehension is very multifaceted and complex. Due to this, readers don't develop an ability to comprehend what is read fast, easy, or independently. These strategies need to be taught over time by teachers and parents that have the experience and knowledge to use them. It may seem when children learn to read in elementary school they can tackle any future words that come their way. This isn't true. Reading comprehension practices have to be practiced, refined, and reinforced constantly through your entire life. During middle and high school, teachers and parents have to help their children increase their reading comprehension strategies. When their reading becomes more challenging, they have to learn new tools in order to understand what they are reading. Materials like journal and magazine articles, newspapers, and textbooks create different challenges for young people and require different strategies. Developing reading comprehension is a process we continue through our entire life that has to change based on the breadth and depth of text they are reading.

Why is comprehension important?

If we don't comprehend what we read, then reading becomes nothing more than looking at letters on a page and trying to sound them out. Think about someone handing you a story written in Ancient Egyptian hieroglyphics and you have no idea about what they mean. You might think they look pretty and might be able to gain some meaning from what you see, but you can't really understand the story. They have no meaning to you. They are just pretty pictures. People read for a lot of reasons and understanding is a big part of the purpose. Comprehending what we read is important since if we can't read, we don't get any information.

Beyond this, comprehension is necessary to live. A lot has been written about how important it is to have a functioning literacy. To be able to thrive and survive in the world today, we have to be able to understand basic words like travel directions, maps, train and bus schedules, directions on packages, transportation documents, purchase contracts, leases, housing agreements, and bills. Comprehension is a crucial component of a functioning literacy. Think about the possibly dire effects of not having the ability to understand the dosage directions on a medicine bottle or warnings on household chemicals. When you can comprehend what you read, we can live productively and safely, we can also continue to develop intellectually, emotionally, and socially.

Speed Reading For Comprehension

There is a huge difference between reading at high speeds and understanding what you have read. We are talking about the difference between reading and comprehension.

This is crucial to any type of reading since we don't usually read just to read. There is no purpose to that. The written language was created as a way to communicate information. The purpose and aim to speed reading is giving you the ability to absorb more information quickly. It lets us obtain information more effectively and efficiently.

There are things called dynamic comprehension and visualization. In other words, when you read, you will form visual pictures, instead of repeating words in your mind, or trying to listen to yourself. If you can handle this, it is extremely effective. If you are reading a novel, you feel like you are in the story. If it is facts that you are reading about, let's say a new vacuum cleaner, the reading might let you see how the device works.

Human beings are visual creatures. Sight is extremely important to us. Language isn't a natural tool but a learned tool. To be able to effectively comprehend during speed reading, you have to translate the words into a language the mind understands which is visualization. If you can accomplish this, you will see that your comprehension level will increase by about 30 percent if not more.

Once you begin to use the technique with speed reading skills, it is best, to begin with, fiction stories instead of non-fiction reports. This is going to build your comprehension skills and visualization. When you begin to feel comfortable visualizing more factual matter, like novels, you can move on to more technical stuff.

Speed reading is a necessity for comprehension and visualization. Speed reading can train the mechanical part of reading so it becomes as effective as possible. The mechanical aspect of reading is what slows down visualization since visualization works at the same speed as our minds. Our minds can be pretty fast. When you can bring your mechanics of reading up to speed with your mind, you will be able to maximize both comprehension and reading. It can triple your reading speed and help you remember what you have just read.

To learn speed reading effectively, you will have to unlearn this habit since it is an artificial one that will slow down your comprehension and reading speed. It is the opposite of how your mind was designed to work which is intuitively, efficiently, and quickly.

If you can find a good speed reading course, along with applying some common sense and intelligence, you will realize that speed reading is intuitive and simple. Speed reading could feel natural and fun.

Speed Reading Myths

You might have seen someone while you were at a library or school that was just breezing through a book. You might have thought that there was no way you would ever be able to read that fast. Some people are just natural readers. Others stumble and take a long time to study and read the same book. Did you stop and wonder why some people can read faster than others but they comprehended more?

Let's look at some of the myths that surround speed reading. You will be able to see it is possible to increase your reading speed, comprehend what you've read, and recall everything you read.

Reading Each Letter Makes a Better Reader

Many people believe that a good read will read every single letter in each word in order to understand what is being read. Look at the bullet point below and see if you can understand it. If you can, this shows your brain can comprehend and decode the words without actually reading every letter in the words. Why are we able to do this? Our brains are wired to look for and understand what is read instead of concentrating on where the letters are placed. Fixating on each letter when reading will just drastically reduce your reading speed. You can learn to speed read and understand what you read without processing each letter.

- "Aocdcnirg to rsecearh at Cmrabdige Uenirvitsy, it dseon't mttear in waht oedrr the ltteers in a wrod are, the olny iprmotnat thing is taht the frist and lsat ltteer be at the rghit pclae.

The rset can be a taotl mses and you can sitll raed it woutiht a porbelm.

Tihs is bcuseae the huamn mnid deos not raed eervy ltteer by istelf, but the wrod as a wohle.

Azamnig huh?"

Reading Slow Creates Better Comprehension

Another silly myth is people think it is easier to concentrate when you read slower. Truthfully, concentration isn't about willpower but reading at the right speed. It is actually hard to pay attention when things are going slower than your thoughts. It is like watching a movie in slow motion. You are going to get bored fast.

With proper training, the brain will be able to read the text in groups instead of just reading every word. This will allow you to read faster and not fixate as much when reading.

Reading Faster Means Lower Comprehension

A lot of people believe that if they read faster it will lessen their ability to understand what they read. Actually having good comprehension depends on if you are able to extract and keep the information that has been read. Some people can read fast and understand well. Others will read slower and comprehend less. We know that speed reading has been proven to increase comprehension.

Reading Slow Means More Enjoyment

Some people think they can only enjoy what they are reading if they read it slowly. The exact opposite is true. Efficiently and effectively speed reading lets the word spring off the page and makes a movie in your mind.

An average person will read at around 150 to 250 words per minute. This is the normal rate a person speaks. They have to reread about 67 percent of what they have already read to comprehend what they read. Reading slower than the speed your brain works at isn't enjoyable.

Reading Faster Means Skipping Words

Another myth is that some words like the, in, at, etc. that have been labeled incorrectly as nonessential can be skipped to be able to read faster. This isn't true. You actually need these words to understand what you are reading.

The bullet point shows how you can't figure out the meaning of the text by leaving out what were thought to be non-essential words.

- "____ truth __ ____ fast _____ ____ skip ____ frequency ____. ____ ____ ____ fixate ____ ____ __ ____. _____ ____, constructing meaning ____ __ difficult."

It is Impossible to Read Faster than 500 WPM

This is so false. Having an ability to talk clearly and fast is harder than being able to read fast.

John Moschitta once held a Guinness World Record for being the fastest speaker. He could speak 586 words per minute. The exercises and techniques to help you learn to speed read are based on having an ability to read more than one word at a time. Being able to read words in groups means we could actually read over 1000 words per minute.

Read Just One Word at a Time

We never read just for words. We read for meanings. We read to get information. We read just for the experience.

The myth is just reading one word at a time goes back to the way we were taught to read. When we were children, our teacher taught us to begin reading individual letters. Then we began to sound out syllables. Next came a complete word. This is when we just stopped. We never moved on from learning letters, syllables, then words, to reading whole phrases, and onto sentences and complete paragraphs. Trying to improve your reading speed will focus on trying to improve the ability to take in and read groups or groupings of many words. Our reading speed is limited because of the way we were taught to read.

Speed Reading Results Won't Last

This can be both false and true. Reading is just a skill like all other skills we've learned over the years. If we don't practice and exercise, it will get a bit rusty. If you spent good money and time to learn to play the piano and then stopped for ten plus years, you are not going to be able to sit down in front of a piano and play "Ammerklavier" by Ludwig Von Beethoven. Good news is when reading, just like with all other skills, to keep sharp, you need to practice occasionally.

Smart People Are the Only Ones Who Read Fast

This, fortunately, isn't true. The main reason we think smart people can read fast is just that they love to read. When you love what you do, you will do it more and will be more sensitive to learning more. It might be people who love to read, actually read fast, and end up smart.

Now you can understand why these myths are totally wrong. You will be better motivated to learn the habits and skill to be an efficient and effective speed reader.

You Can't Enjoy Reading

Many people think that when you speed read you don't enjoy reading. I beg to differ. Speed reading is reading efficiently. If you can speed read, you are a better reader. You will get more meaning and pleasure out of websites, articles, and books you read. Most people love to read after they have learned to speed read.

Pointer

The easiest way to increase your reading speed is to use a pointing device. It can be a pen or just your finger. Using something to help move your eyes across the page could create an immediate boost to your reading speed.

This happens because your eyes are like a cat. Any type of movement will attract them. When you use a pointer, it helps improve your reading speed by pulling your eyes across the page. You are just moving the pointer from the left to the right and line by line. Sounds simple, right?

Reading while using a pointer will improve your focus. It can be hard to focus while you read. Everyone's lives are full of distractions that take our focus away from reading. Think about what it would have been like to read 100 years ago. There wouldn't have been any distractions from text messages or phone calls. There wouldn't have been any urges to check Facebook or email. But in this day and age, distractions are all around us.

How in the world can we get rid of these distractions easily? First of all, the easiest way to get rid of these distractions would be turning off your computer or phone. Second, using a pointer to guide your eyes when you read will improve your focus. This will also improve how well you comprehend what you are reading. This simple technique is the main concept in every speed reading course.

Pencil Pointer

When you first attempt to lead your eyes, use a pencil to guide you as you read. In order to not mark up the page, use the eraser end of the pencil. You might want to use a ball point pen or another object. Make sure the pen isn't clicked on.

Find a book and open it. The objective is to read two pages using a pen or pencil as a pointer. While you are reading, just glide the pencil across the page below the words you are reading. Read normally. Once you reach the end of a line, move the pencil to the beginning of the next line. Read once again at a normal pace.

Take a break and allow your eyes to rest. Once your eyes feel rested, read the next three pages using the pointer again.

Hand Pointer

This will be just like using a pencil but you will be using your index finger. Close your hand into a relaxed fist with your index finger pointing out. Don't clench your fist tightly closed or it might cause your hand to begin to cramp. Relax your hand even more but keep the other fingers tucked under your palm.

Grab your favorite book and glide your finger across a line. The words you are reading should be right above your finger. This hand position is comfortable for most people but if you find it uncomfortable, you can change it up by flattening your hand and using your middle finger as the guide. You can experiment with hand positions until you find one that works best for you. Just make sure your hands are relaxed and comfortable.

Open your book again. You are going to read the next three pages and use your finger as the pointing tool. While reading, just glide your finger across the page with the words right above the finger. Read normally. Once you have reached the end of a line, move your finger to the beginning of the next line. Read again at a normal pace.

Once you are done reading the three pages, take a break and let your eyes rest. Once your eyes feel rested, read the next three pages using the same method.

Do these practices twice each day for a week until you feel comfortable using your finger as a pointer.

Fast Return

For the exercises above when you got to the end of the line, you moved your pointer down to the next line at a normal pace. The time you move down to the next line, you aren't reading at all. This will reduce your reading speed. When you minimize the return time, you will be making a positive difference on your reading speed. In the next practice, try to move your pointer to the next line as fast as you can. Then read the text at a normal speed. You will use this technique for the rest of these practices.

Open a book. The main objective is to read three pages using your finger as a pointer. While reading, glide your finger so it is just below the word you are reading. Read at a normal pace. Once you reach the end, move your finger down to the next line as fast as you can. Read normally.

Page Turning

Once you have reached the end of a page, you can lessen the time it takes you to start reading the next one. If you are reading the left-hand page, just move your finger to the top of the right-hand page as fast as you can and start reading normally. If you are at the end of the right-hand page, use your left hand to lessen the time it takes to turn the page.

When you are reading a left-hand page, put your left hand so it is holding the book comfortably. You are holding the book open with both hands right now.

When you are reading the right-hand page, put your left hand on top of the right-hand page right at the edge of the book. When you are approaching the bottom of the right-hand page, push against the page slightly using a finger of your left hand. This will make the page raise up just a bit from the rest of the book. When you have finished that page, grasp the page with your left hand and turn it quickly in one clean stroke. Put your right hand at the top of the left-hand page and start reading normally. Do this for the rest of the practices.

If you are left-handed, experiment with the above technique until it feels right for you.

Open your book. The next objective is to read four pages using your finger as the pointing tool. When you get to the end of a line, move your finger to the beginning of the next line as fast as you can. Once you have gotten to the bottom of the left-hand page, move your finger to the top of the right-hand page as fast as you can. Take your left hand and turn the page as it was described earlier. Read normally.

Repeat this two times a day for the next week to get familiar with using the pointing and turning method.

Now we are going to add a timing sheet and see how long it takes you to finish this exercise. Open your book. You are going to read six pages doing the same things as above. Remember to read at your normal pace. You can find timing sheets on the internet. Just do an internet search for speed reading timing sheets.

Since you have been using your finger as a pointer, you are making it easier for your eyes to flow across the page. Your eyes follow motion naturally. You have done this without realizing it when you saw something move out of the corner of your eye, you automatically turned toward it. You might one day be able to do this without using a pointing tool, but for now get your eyes used to following something.

Let's do another exercise. Use another timing sheet and time yourself. You are going to do the exact same thing as you did above. When you are finished, fill out the sheet to see your progress. You might be able to already see you are getting better at increasing your reading speed.

What to do if you are reading on a computer?

If you do a lot of reading on a computer, you probably don't want to place your hand on your computer screen. Here are some ways to work around this scenario. If your computer has an external mouse, you can just move the mouse's cursor across your computer's screen as you read. This will help your eyes move easily across the screen. If you are using a laptop, this probably won't be as useful since a laptop's mouse will actually make it harder to move the cursor.

If you read a lot on a computer, there is a great speed reading program that is free. It is called AccelaReader. It is easy to use and lets you read faster on a computer screen. The technology that runs it is called Rapid Serial Visual Presentation or RSVP Reading. These types of programs are perfect for people who use a computer to read a lot.

Here is how this program works. The first thing

you do is copy and paste the text you want to read into the box of the app. Then set the speed that you want to read at. Last, click on the read button and the app will flash words on the screen at the desired speed.

You can make some adjustments like how many words you want to be flashed at one time. It is recommended to set it where two words are flashed at one time. You can add more when you get more used to the app. The font size can also be adjusted to a color and size that works for you.

Is there a way to read faster when using a tablet?

It is hard to use your hand to guide your eyes when you read on a tablet because of the problems with a touchscreen. One way to help you read faster with a tablet is setting up some points of fixation on each line. Try to make two fixation points for each line by using your eyes. Try to imagine the line of text has been broken in half. As you read, you will need to fixate on each half. When you fixate on the first half, try to read the words as a group when you see them.

If there are very long lines with more than 12 words on a line, you might need to break it down into three fixations on each line. Place one at the start, one middle ways, and one at the end. After some practice, you will begin to notice how much easier it gets to read groups of words by just glancing. A lot of people read words by using fixations on every word they see. Fixating on each word will make reading tedious and slow.

To Sum it Up

To read faster, try to use a pointer when you read. You need to take advantage of the fact you eyes get attracted to movement. This is a great way to do that. If you practice the exercises described above, you are now able to decrease the time it takes you to turn a page and get to the next line. You will soon realize you are reading faster and your focus is better. Your comprehension will start getting better when reading with a pointer.

Stop Subvocalizing

When you were taught to read, a teacher told you to say each word out loud. When you became fluent enough, another teacher told you to begin saying the words in your head. This is when we learned how to subvocalize. Most people will read this way their entire lives. If you want to read faster, you have to get rid of that habit.

You don't have to say each word in your head to understand what you read. When you are young, it is necessary to say every word, but since you can understand the word just by seeing it, you don't need to say them to yourself.

There might be situations where you can read without speaking the word in your head. Think about driving. When you see a stop sign, you don't actually say the word "STOP" in your head.

You see it and recognize it as a stop sign. You know what to do.

As with most readers, everyone subvocalizes all the words in their head. You don't have to subvocalize every word you see. If you are reading and saw the year "1968", you most likely aren't going to say "nineteen sixty-eight" in your head. You are going to understand the year just be seeing it. If you were to see the number "7,792,832,742" you aren't going to say the words "seven billion, seven hundred ninety-two million, eight hundred thirty-two thousand, seven hundred and forty-two". That is just too much. When you see a number like that, you know it is a big one. You understand that fast. You don't subvocalize it. If you did, you would stare at it for a while without making it through the complete sentence.

It's Not about Words but Ideas

Reading isn't about words but about finding ideas, getting details, and absorbing information.

Words don't mean much if they aren't surrounded by other words. When you see the words Las Vegas, do you even realize it is two separate words? Most people don't even think about it as two separate words.

Many words we see and just there for grammatical purposes. They don't give you the same meaning like words like university do. We must lessen subvocalization to be able to boost our reading. Why? Because saying every word in our head limits the speed at which we read.

Think about this: if you say each word, this means you are only reading as fast as you talk. If you say each word in your head, your limit is your talking speed.

Reading Speed is Talking Speed

An average reading speed is around 150 to 200 words per minute. The average talking speed is the same. How? Most people say words to themselves while reading. They usually read at the same rate as they talk. You can test this for yourself if you want. Try reading normally for one minute. Then read out loud for one minute. If you are like most, your reading and talking speed will be close. It will be within about 50 words lower or higher.

If you read faster than you talk, that's a good thing. We don't want our talking speed to limit us.

Why do we read around 150 to 250 words per minute and not above 300? It is too hard to talk that fast. That is unless you do the disclaimers at the end of commercials. It is difficult to talk over 300 words per minute. Our subvocalization needs to be minimized since we don't want to be able to read at the same speed as we talk. You can read as fast as you think.

Changing this habit is going to be hard since we can't just turn off this voice. Instead of totally getting rid of the habit, we need to minimize it. Keep in mind there are many words in sentences and paragraphs that are not needed to get the meaning of a paragraph. You read for ideas instead of words.

It is Useful

Saying words silently could be helpful at times. If the material you are reading is technical or vocabulary you don't know. In these situations, saying the words in your head, or out loud, is useful to expand or improve vocabulary.

If you need to memorize a poem word for word, subvocalizing or saying them out loud will help. This is how professionals learn their lines. Reading out loud will help you memorize it word for word. When you read normally, you don't need to know everything word for word. You are reading for information, details, and ideas.

To increase your reading speed, you have to minimize subvocalization by saying just a few words on each line. If you go for every word, you are limiting your speed.

How are you going to know if you have made progress? If you begin reading 300 words per minute, you aren't saying each word in your head. If you go over 400 words per minute, you are making progress and are just saying a few words in your head.

The best way to begin speed reading and break old habits is to begin reading with your eyes.

There are five ways this can be done:

Use a Guide

Use a finger or pen to drag your eyes across the page. Instead of just using your eyes to follow the text, use a pointer. It doesn't matter if it is a pen or finger; just use it to drag your eyes across the text. Put the pointer under the line you are reading, begin moving it across the text. When you first begin, move it at the same time as your eyes in their normal reading. Now, slowly begin to increase the pointer and make your eyes catch up.

This is going to take practice but you will quickly figure out that when you are dragging the pointer faster than you normally read, you will still understand everything you read.

This is an important step when speed reading. Begin doing this when you read any type of non-fiction. By dragging your eyes with a pointer, you will begin proving to your brain that it has the ability to move faster. You will find it impossible to subvocalize as fast as you are dragging the pointer.

This is the key. For three days in a row, use a pointer every time you read and follow the pointer with your eyes instead of the other way around.

Drown It Out

This is the most important step when speed reading, and it is the weirdest. You have to understand that hearing what you are reading has nothing to do with understanding them. Your brain has the capability to turn text into meaning with an internal monologue. This monologue is disrupting the way you comprehend.

The next step: After you are comfortable following a pointer, begin counting to three in your head over and over. You can begin doing this out loud if it helps you at first. Continue to follow the pointer with your eyes and try to understand the text. NEVER stop counting to three.

If you fill your mind with counting, your brain isn't going to be able to subvocalize what you are reading. You are going to begin absorbing the information automatically instead of the old way that you used to do.

This may seem strange at first but after a few tries, you will realize you are comprehending the material just like you used to without having to hear what you are reading in your head. You will be reading a lot faster, too.

You have to keep practicing this process because bad habits are very hard to break. You have been reading the other way your whole life. You have to keep dragging that pointer and drowning your subvocalization until you feel comfortable doing this. These are going to take your speed reading to a whole new level.

Listen to Music

This helps you minimize subvocalization and it can help you concentrate better. Remember that not all kinds of music will help you concentrate. You are going to want to stay away from listening to music that has lyrics or a strong beat. This will throw off your concentration. You want to stay away from songs that remind you of things like your favorite movie, high school sweetheart, etc.

Listen to instrumental music. Classical music is the best. This helps you improve concentration and minimize subvocalization.

Use AccelaReader RSVP App

This will help boost your reading speed while minimizing subvocalization. The app is easy to use. You just paste the text you want into a box. Set the reading speed and push play. The words will blink on the screen at the speed you preset. You could also choose the number of words you want to read at one time.

The recommended setting is 300 words per minute. Anything above that will help you avoid saying all words. The faster you can go the fewer words you will subvocalize. With practice, you will find it easier to minimize this habit.

Force Yourself to Read Faster

If you normally read at 250 words per minute, try to go a bit faster at about 300. If you can force yourself to go a bit faster than normal, you are going to minimize the number of words you subvocalize. In addition to this, you will improve focus because you are paying more attention when you read faster. Remember the more you practice, the faster you will get.

To Sum it Up

Many programs for speed reading usually exaggerate the possibility by claiming that you can totally eliminate subvocalization. Your goal needs to be trying to minimize the habit and not eliminating it. The tips above will help you minimize the habit so you can begin reading faster.

Scanning

Scanning and skimming are techniques for reading that use keywords and rapid eye movement to quickly move through text for different reasons. Each of them is used for different purposes. They aren't meant to be used at all times. They are on the fast end of the range of speed reading while studying is at the slow end. Skimming is rapidly reading so you can get a feel for the material. Scanning is rapidly reading so you can find certain facts. Skimming will give you information in a certain section, scanning will help you find a specific fact. Skimming is like snorkeling and scanning for pearls.

People who can scan and skim are considered flexible readers. They will read whichever way they need to for a certain purpose to get information without wasting time. They never read each word and this helps to increase their reading speed. They have the skill to know what certain information they need to read and which method they need to use.

You can use skimming to preview which is reading before actually reading. You can use skimming to review which is reading after you have already read. You can use skimming to determine the main idea of long material you don't want to read. You can use skimming to find certain material for research papers.

You can use scanning to research and find specific facts, to answer a question that requires support from facts, and to study materials that are fact heavy.

Skimming

Skimming is a tool you can use to read more material in less time. It can save you many hours of reading. This isn't the best way to read. It's useful to use it as a preview for more detailed reading or if you need to review a lot of content. When skimming, you might miss points that were important or overlook meanings that were obscured.

When you skim, you are only looking for main or general ideas. It works best when reading non-fiction materials. You focus on what's important for your purpose. Skimming happens when you read and lets you look for details along with the main ideas.

A lot of people think skimming is haphazard and places the eyes where they fall. In order to skim effectively, you need structure but don't read every single word. The words you read are more important than the ones you leave out. How do you determine what to read and what not to read?

If you are doing research on a website, reading the first few paragraphs will get you an idea of what information is being discussed.

When skimming, you need to prepare yourself to move quickly through all the pages. Don't read each word. Just pay attention to heading, bold or italic type, indented, numbered or bulleted lists. Stay alert for key phrases and words, words you aren't familiar with, nouns, dates, places, and names. Try to follow these guidelines:

- Read the chapter overview or table of contents to figure out the main ideas.

- Look at the headings of each chapter to see if any words pop out at you. Read the headings of any tables and charts.

- Read the whole introductory paragraph and then just the first sentence and last sentence in each paragraph. In every paragraph, read just the first few words of the sentence to get the main idea.

- Quickly read any sentence that contains keywords that are either italicized or boldface.

- If you found something you think is significant, read the whole sentence just to make sure. Then continue in the same manner. Don't let temptation get the better of you don't read any details you aren't looking for.

- If there are chapter summaries, read them.

After you realize where the material is heading, you can just read the first sentence in every paragraph. This is called topic sentences and it will give you the paragraph's main ideas. If you don't get the main idea in the first sentence or if the paragraph sucks you in, you might want to skim more.

Keep reading only the topic sentences and dropping down the rest of the paragraphs until you are close to the end. The last few paragraphs might hold a summary or conclusion. You need to stop skimming and read the rest in detail. Your comprehension is going to be lower than if you read in detail. While you are skimming, if you think you are getting the main idea, then you are doing it correctly.

Skimming helps you quickly locate information while using your time wisely. It also increases the usable material you comprehend for research.

Let's say you have a big test in a couple days. You want to review the material but don't want to reread all of it. When you skim, you will be able to locate the information you haven't mastered and can just study that.

You can ask yourself these questions while reading to help you figure out whether or not you should skim. If your answer to any is yes, then skimming would be useful:

- Can you skip any of the material?

- Do you already know a little bit about this?

- Is there a lot to read and not a lot of time?

- Is it non-fiction material?

If you have some prior knowledge or don't think it's important, then skip it. Yes, don't read it. Skipping material might be the best way to use your time. Just because somebody wrote something down doesn't mean you are obligated to read it. If you can pick and choose what you skip and skim, you will be surprised at the amount of information you will be able to get through quickly.

Good skimmers won't skim everything. They won't even give the same attention to everything. Skimming is faster than normal reading. You need to slow down in these situations:

- When skimming concluding and introductory paragraphs.

- When skimming topic sentences.

- If you find a word you don't understand.

- If the material is complicated.

Scanning for Research

Scanning is another tool to help you increase your reading speed. It is different than skimming because you just look of a certain fact or piece of information without completely reading all words.

Scanning also uses organizational cues and keywords. When you skim, you just get a bird's eye view of materials. When scanning, you are trying to find then hold onto certain facts.

You probably scan more than you think you do. You are scanning when looking for your favorite television shows on the cable guide. You scan when you are looking for a friend's number in your telephone book. You scan when you look at sports scored in the paper. In order to be successful when scanning, you have to know how the material is structured and are able to comprehend what you are reading so you will be able to find the information needed. Scanning lets you locate information and details quickly.

First, figure out what you are researching, locate the right material, and know how the structure of the information is before you begin scanning.

Facts might be buried inside a very long passage of material that doesn't have much to do with the topic you are researching. Skim this first to see if it might contain the material you need. Remember to look at typographical cues, headings, indexes, summaries, and tables of contents. In order to understand the tables and lists, skim first to see how well they are organized whether it is most to least, chronological, or alphabetical.

The information might also be arranged in a non-alphabetical order like parts in an auto parts catalog, television listings, or category. Information might be located inside paragraphs of text or textual sense like in encyclopedias.

After you have skimmed, figure out if the material is useful. If it is, proceed to scan:

- You need to know what you are looking for. Figure out some keywords or phrases to look for. You are going to be the search engine.

- Scan for just one keyword at a time. If you try to use multiples, you are just going to get confused. If there is more than one thing you are looking for, do several scans.

- Allow your eyes to go quickly down a page until you find the phrase or words you want.

- If your eye catches a keyword, read the material carefully.

Using your hands when scanning is useful when trying to find certain information. If you run your finger down a dictionary page to find a word, to locate a meeting on the calendar, to read a bus or train schedule, this helps to focus your attention and keeps your place when scanning columns of material.

Peripheral vision is also a helpful scanning tool. As your finger moves down a list, you are not only seeing the name your finger is at but the names below and above it. Allow your eyes to work for you when scanning.

Scanning for Answers

If you are looking for information to answer certain questions, the most important step has been done for you. The question gives you the keywords you need to look for. Follow these steps to help you find the answers:

- Completely read every question before you begin scanning. Choose the keywords from the question.

- Concentrate on just one question at a time. Scan for each question separately.

- Once you have located a keyword, carefully read the surrounding text to see if anything is relevant.

- Read the question again to see if the answer you found actually answers your question.

Keep your keyword in mind while you are scanning. When do you need to scan? When your goal is to locate certain information. If you are researching material for a presentation, you can scan the book's index, reference materials, and websites. You can discover if they contain the information you need and what page they are located on.

You have probably scanned without even realizing what you were doing. With this information, you should be able to use scanning more frequently and intentionally. The more you do this, the more effective your scanning will be. The best benefit of scanning is the ability to help you be a better reader. Scanning will add another gear to your reading.

Humans have been geared to read every word on a page and it might be hard to leave words out. You have to allow yourself to overlook words by skipping, scanning, and skimming material. It all depends on what you need. You have permission not to read every word on a page.

Scanning requires concentration and can be tiring. You might need to practice at keeping your attention on the material and not letting it wander. Pick a place and time that will work for you and then dive right in.

Eye Exercises

The muscles in your eyeballs and eye sockets control your eye movements, and like all other muscles in your body, you can strengthen these through different exercises. This eye strength is helpful when you want to speed read, which taxes your eyes more than a regular reading speed because it will require you to cover more space on a page. When you make your eye muscles stronger and flexible, it will improve your vision clarity and will slow down natural eyesight deterioration that happens with aging.

Before you start your speed reading training, it is important that you train your eye muscles. This will help to expand your visual field. This type of training is meant to help you to read faster and to help you make faster connections with the things you read. While things may not go all that great at first, it is important that you practice all of this over and over again until you can increase your speed.

Fun fact, humans have the weakest peripheral vision range than any other species.

Eye Training

This is probably the hardest exercise you will have to do because it is all about speed. Make sure you go at a comfortable speed at first and don't allow yourself to get dizzy. The more you do it, the faster you will be able to go.

1. Start by staring off in the distance then start to move your eyes up and down as quickly as you can. Do this for ten seconds.

2. Once the ten seconds are up, let your eyes rest for a second and then move them from left to right as quickly as you can. Again, do this for ten seconds.

3. Rest for a few seconds, and then repeat this process three more times.

This exercise works your lower and upper oblique muscles. When you do this at high speeds, you will start to sense light and colors. For example, you may start to see stars in the middle of what you are looking at. This will cause your brain's five senses to wake up. You will feel a warm sensation, different smells, and you may even feel some pain.

Through this repetition, the sensory faculties of your right brain will begin to surface. Through rhythmically training your eyes at these high speeds, you will start to evoke images of form, light, and color. This will help you with speed reading

Thumb-to-thumb glancing

This method of eye exercise works the muscles in the eye sockets that work your peripheral vision and it helps to stretch the muscles in general so that they are more flexible and healthier.

In order to get the most from this exercise, you

need to try and glance at both of your thumbs without allowing your head to move.

1. Sit or stand and look straight out in front of you, stretch your arms out to the side at shoulder length and then stick your thumbs up.

2. Without allowing your head to move glance between your right and left thumb ten times.

3. Repeat this process three times.

The first few times you do this your head may hurt a bit, and you may find it hard to keep from moving your head. This will get easier the more you do it.

Infinity Loop or Figure Eight

This is a perfect exercise to strengthen your eye muscles. This helps improve your eyes' flexibility. Here is how this exercise is performed:

1. Pretend that there is a giant figure of the

number eight (8) in front of you at around ten feet.

2. Now, move the figure eight so that it is on its side.

3. Now, trace this sideways figure eight with your eyes in a very slow motion.

4. Perform the in one direction for a few minutes and then trace for a few minutes in the other direction.

Eye Writing

This exercise will have you moving your eyes in ways that they don't normally move, which gives them a pretty good workout. This exercise works the extra-ocular muscles in your eye socket and it great for increasing your eye's range of motion and eyeball flexibility. This exercise could not be any easier:

1. Stare at a wall that is located on the other side of the room. Try to use the wall that is

the farthest from you.

2. Pretend that you are writing out your name on that wall using only your eyes. Basically, you should move your eyes in the shape of the letters in your name. Act as if you are using a paintbrush to write your name on that wall. You can start out writing your name in block letters and then do it in cursive.

This will be hard at first, but the more you do it the easier it will get. The first time you do it, it may not even feel like you're doing anything.

Hooded Eyes

This exercise is meant to relax your eyes. This exercise should be done two to three times whenever your eyes are in need of a little timeout.

1. Shut your eyes about halfway and then focus on stopping your eyelids from shaking. While you are concentrating on what your eyelids are doing, you are

allowing your eyes to relax.

2. While you still have your eyes half closes, gaze at something that is far away from you. This will make your eyes stop trembling.

Just like all of the other exercise, you will have to practice this a few times before it feels like you are doing things correctly.

Zooming

This is a perfect exercise when you want to work on the way your eyes focus. With this exercise, you will be constantly adjusting your focus length. This will strengthen up the muscles in your eyes. Here is how to perform zooming:

1. Sit up in a comfortable position with your feet flat on the floor.

2. Stretch your arms out in front of you with your thumbs up in a hitchhiking position.

3. Now, focus your eyes on your thumbs with

your arms outstretched.

4. Now slowly move your thumbs closer to you and keep your focus on your thumbs until they are almost three inches in front of your face.

5. You will then move your thumbs backward again, still focusing your eyes on your thumbs, until they are fully outstretched.

6. Repeat this for a few minutes at different times during the day.

Eye Squeezes

These eye squeezes will also help to relax your eyes, will make the muscles more flexible, and it helps to increase the blood and oxygen flow to your faces and eyes. This should take you around three minutes to do.

1. While you inhale slowly and deeply, open your mouth and eyes as wide as you

possibly can and let all of the muscles in your face stretch out.

2. While you exhale, close and squeeze your eyes as tight as you can as you are squeezing the other muscles in your head, face, and neck and clenching your jaw shut.

3. Hold in your breath as you are squeezing everything for 30 seconds.

4. Repeat this process four more times. After that, take a short break and then repeat this five more times.

This is a really fun exercise to do. If you are feeling rather tense, this is a great way to release it, plus you get to make a funny face. Although, if you are in an office setting or in public, you may want to find a private spot so that you don't freak anybody out.

Around the World

Not only is this great for getting your eyes ready to speed read, but this exercise can help prevent presbyopia, which will happen when the elasticity of your eyes start to deteriorate because of the lack of eye movement. When this happens, you will find it harder to focus on things at different distances. This is how to perform around the world:

1. Make sure you are sitting comfortably or standing in an area that is generally traffic-free.

2. Close both of your eyes, or you can leave them open, but make sure that your head doesn't move at all while you are doing the following movements with your eyes.

3. Roll your eyes up, as if you are looking up, and leave them there for three seconds, and then roll your eyes down and hold that for three seconds. If you have chosen to

keep your eyes open, wait until your eyes have focused on a certain object before you move your eyes to the next exercise.

4. Now, look to the far right and hold this for three seconds and then look as far left as you can and hold this for three seconds.

5. Now look up to the top left and hold this for three seconds and then look to the top right and hold for three seconds.

6. Lastly, rotate your eyes clockwise two times and the counterclockwise for two rotations.

Change Focus

This one will help strength how your eyes focus on the object. You will be alternating between close and far away objects in this exercise, so you may notice that your head starts to hurt the first few times you do this.

1. Look up from what you are currently looking at and focus on something in the distance.

2. Then look at something close up again.

3. Repeat this a few times, or until your eyes start to feel refreshed.

This is also sometimes called 20/20/20. This is because that you need to take a break every 20 minutes to look at something that is 20 feet away for 20 seconds. This is supposed to help prevent eye strain.

Palm Your Eyes

This is the easiest exercise there is, and it is exactly as it sounds.

1. Rub the palms of your hands together briskly to help warm them up a bit.

2. Put the palms of your hands over your closed eyes and then gently rub the bony spots around your eyes. Make sure you

157

don't rub directly on your eyeballs. Do this for about 30 seconds.

3. With your palms still covering your eyes, open up your eyes and create a seal around your eyes. You should be looking into complete darkness. Stay here for a moment or two.

Clock Gazing

1. Sit in a comfortable position with a straight spine and both of your feet on the floor.

2. Picture a giant clock face about a foot in front of you.

3. Keeping your head completely still, look at where the 12 would be, then you will look down at where the six would be. You will continue in this manner:

   a. One to seven.

   b. Two to eight.

158

c. Three to nine.

d. Four to 10.

e. Five to 11.

4. After you finish, close your eyes and let them rest for about 30 seconds.

When you close your eyes, this would be a good time to palm your eyes if you would like.

Speed Reading Tips

Most people read some sort of material every day. They might browse a book, look through files at work, or skim through a blog post. Reading through huge passages of text is hard on the eyes, mentally exhausting, and time-consuming. If you would like to read faster and remember what you read, here are some tips that might help you achieve this:

- Do a Text Preview: When you see the trailer for the next action-packed movie before you watch it, it will give you some context clues and will allow you to understand what to expect. This is similar to previewing text before you read. It gives you a quick understanding of what you will be reading. In order to preview text, look at it from start to finish. Pay attention to bullet points, large or bold fonts, subheading, and headings. In order to get a better understanding, look over the introduction and conclusion paragraphs. Look for transition sentences. Look at any graphs or images. Try to figure out the structure of the text.

- Plan of Attack: Approaching the text strategically will change how well you can understand the material. First, think about what goal you are trying to achieve. What is it you want to learn from reading this material? Write down any questions that you would like answered when you finish. Figure out what goal the author was trying to come to. Base this on your preview. The author might have wanted to give you the whole history of Ancient Rome. Your goal is just to answer a question about women's roles in Roman politics. If the goal you have is more limited than the author's, try to find the sections that have what you are looking for and just read these. You might have to change up your plan of attack according to the kind of material you are going to be reading. If you have to read a science text or huge legal paper, you probably need to only read specific passages carefully and slowly.

- Be Mindful: Being able to read fast and comprehend what you have just read takes concentration and focus. Try to eliminate any interruptions, distractions, and noise. Be mindful if your thoughts begin to wander while you read. If you begin to fantasize about what you are going to eat instead of what you are reading, bring your mind gently back to the text. Most readers will read some sentences without actually focusing on them. They then go back and read the same passage again until they understand what they are reading. This is called regression and it will slow you down and it will be harder to figure out what the big picture is of the text. If you can attentively and carefully approach the text, you will realize whether or not you understand a section. This will save you a bunch of time.

- Never Read All Sections: It is a myth that students have to read each section in an article or textbook. If you aren't reading something that is extremely important, skip over the sections that don't pertain to your purpose. Selectively reading makes it possible for you to understand the important points of most texts, instead of just being able to read a few of them.

- Create a Summary: Your job isn't over once you have read the last word. Once you have finished reading, write out a summary of what you have read. See if you can answer the questions you had before you began reading. Did you learn what you wanted to? When you take some time after you have finished reading, combine the data, and write down what you have learned, you are going to put the material in your brain and will be able to recall it later. If you are a verbal or a visual learner, draw a summary or tell somebody about what you have learned.

- Do Timed Runs: Strategically approaching the text, actively reading, and then effectively writing a summary takes some practice. To improve reading speed, set a timer and see how many words you can read per minute. As you increase your reading speed, check in and make sure you are happy with how well you comprehend what you are reading.

- Read Early: A lot of people are able to improve their comprehension and even double their reading speed if they will read the material early in the day.

- Prioritize Reading: Make three piles to put the materials you have to read in. These should be least important, moderately important, and very important. Read them in order of their importance. You will be amazed at how well you will improve your reading speed. This will also improve how well you comprehend the material. This happens because you are reading the very important material first when your mind is sharp and clear.

- Create a Question: You will greatly improve the way you comprehend your reading, speed of reading, and concentrating on what you are reading by looking at the subheadings and headings in the material you are reading. Turn these into questions and look quickly for an answer. You will increase your reading speed when you do this. You will be more focused on what you are reading.

- Read in the Right Environment: If you can, prop your reading material on a bookstand. When you can place your reading material at a 45-degree angle, it will reduce eyestrain and increase your reading speed. Try not to read important or difficult material in the bed. This will prevent you from relaxing your body and mind. You are going to stay more alert when you sit at a desk.

- Create a Course of Action: You can increase your reading speed and keep from having to re-read material by taking notes right after you have read each piece of material. Look back at your notes for each piece when you need to refer back to the text later.

- Don't Highlight: Even though readers think that highlighting text will increase their reading speed and how well they comprehend what they read. The reverse is really true. Highlighting just means they aren't bothering to learn what they are reading at this moment. The end result is they are going to read the material twice and then they might not remember or understand even then.

- Have Flexible Reading Speeds: There are just some materials that have to be read carefully and slowly like poetry, math equations, and legal contracts. Other materials could be read at faster speeds like novels, magazines, and newspapers. Adjust your speed to the kind of material you are reading and the purpose of reading.

- Stop Rereading: The biggest taker of time is when reading stopping and rereading what you have just read. You do this because you don't understand what you've just read or you want to understand it better. Many think that if you don't understand each word or line of text, the whole article isn't going to make sense. You will eventually realize that you aren't gaining any comprehension when you reread.

- Read More: Reading is a skill that will take time to develop. You will get better the more you do. Reading isn't a race but the more time you can set aside for reading, the better you will get. The better you get, the faster you read. The best way to enjoy a great novel is to read at your own pace but when you are dealing with technical aspects, speed reading will get you through the material faster.

- Word-Chunking: When you chunk words together you are really just reading multiple words at one time. It is the main key to reading faster. It can sometimes be hard to retrain the brain to stop reading every word. Focus on reading three words at a time. Continue through the page and take note of how much faster you have gone through the page. You can still comprehend and process everything you have read. You are just spending less time doing it. To learn to do this better, take a pencil and draw two parallel, vertical lines down the page so that you have separated the page into three sections. Begin at the top left of the page like normal. Cover up everything that is below that line. Try to read the chunks of text in every section as one thing. Chunk them together just like you would read a road sign. Continue going down the page. You will see that you are already reading faster.

- Use Peripheral Vision: This is the main step that ties all of these things together. Read as you normally would but this time you are going to concentrate on the center of the line. Use your peripheral vision to read the remainder. Scan the page like this and once you have reached the end. You will realize you understood everything you read but you read it extremely fast.

- Improve Your Vocabulary: When you are reading and you come to a word you don't know what do you do? Skip it? Figure it out with context clues? Take time to look it up? Whatever you do, you are slowing down your reading, if you don't stop it at all. If you can improve your vocabulary, you are going to know more words. The more words you can add to your vocabulary, the faster you are going to read. The faster you can read, the more you are able to read. It might be self-explanatory, but it is important.

- Outline Text: You aren't going to need to use a paper and pencil. This can be done in your head. If what you are reading is a dense report or news article. Just read the first two paragraphs of the text to get an idea of its main points. Now, jump down to every paragraph and just read the first sentence.

- Read Actively: To be able to do this engage fully in the text. What do you want to get out of what you are reading? If what you are reading isn't what you need to completely commit to, just jump over it. If your mind wanders, it is going to make your reading slower.

- Enjoy What You Are Reading: This is a wonderful way to develop your skills naturally and faster. The more you enjoy what you do the more you will do it.

- Keep a Chart: If you can track your progress on a chart it will greatly motivate you to continue reading. Take a test every now and then to calculate how fast you are reading. Keep track of these changes on a chart to help you see how improved your reading speed has gotten. Looking back at your progress can be very rewarding.

- Get Rid of Boredom: If you have ever tried to read something and get bored or end up daydreaming after reading a sentence that sent you down a rabbit hole. You must get rid of these pauses. It will help you finish your reading a lot faster. Find an interest that will link you to the material. Find a link to the book you are reading to something that interests you. You might also need to find a better location to read in. If you get sleepy or bored when you read in your bedroom, try to read outside, in a coffee shop, or in a library.

- Keep Your Mouth Busy: Many readers like to read their words either out loud or silently. If you can stop this, you will be able to read faster. You can prevent this by keeping your mouth busy doing something else while reading. If your mouth is humming, sucking, or chewing, it keeps your vocal cords busy and keeps your brain for saying the words it sees. When you preoccupy your mouth, you are freeing your mind to read faster.

Conclusion

Thank for making it through to the end of *Speed Reading*, let's hope it was informative and able to provide you with all of the tools you need to achieve your goals whatever they may be.

The next step is to find out what your current reading speed is a go from there. Pick your favorite techniques and get started increasing your reading speed. You never know when this sill will come in handy and make your life a lot easier. Get started today.

Finally, if you found this book useful in any way, a review on Amazon is always appreciated!

Description

Have you ever wished that you could read a book faster? Are you tired of not comprehending what you read?

Well, look no further. This is the book you need. Speed reading is real and it can help you in nearly every aspect of your life. A lot of people think that speed reading takes away from the reading process, but it actually adds to it. Those who speed read understand more of what they read than average readers.

This book will cover things such as:

- The history of speed reading.

- The benefits of speed reading.

- How you can test your current reading speed.

- Several speed reading techniques.

- The way the human mind works.

- Fixing any current problems you have with reading.

Stop slowly making your way through books. Learn how to increase your reading speed and improve the way your mind works. Speed reading is a great skill to have; you never know when it is going to come in handy. Don't wait any longer. Get this book today and start reading faster now.

Printed in Great Britain
by Amazon

32828483R00106